When Your Child Discloses
Sexual Abuse:
A Step-By-Step Guide for Parents

Chris Schopen, MA, LPC

To Kenneth, my Companion of the Heart: without you, none of this would have been possible.

CONTENTS

SECTION 4
THE SEXUAL ABUSE DISCLOSURE'S IMPACT ON YOU

SECTION 5
HELPFUL TIDBITS

ACKNOWLEDGMENTS

My husband, Kenneth, without whose support, nothing in my life would be of import!

My family for always being my biggest cheerleaders and critics, of which I've always needed both!

My dearest friends, Marina, Rachel, and Adriana for always being my sounding board!

My friend and photographer, Jenny Farley of JenAnnCreative Photography, who turns photos into more than a thousand words!

Kim Eldredge of NewFrontierBooks.com – my publisher, editor, and the spark that fueled my book-writing fire!

Nada, my illustrator, who truly understands how to artistically express the sentiment behind the words on the page!

FOREWORD

My child told me that someone has sexually abused him. What do I do now? This is a question so many parents have asked me over the twenty plus years that I have prosecuted people who have committed sexual crimes against children. It is a question that no parent ever expects to have to ask—but many find themselves asking. It is a question that must be answered at a time when you are experiencing a flood of emotions: anger at the abuser, guilt as a parent, fear for your child's physical and emotional health and future, fear of what may happen next and even grief over the loss of relationships with people who may support the abuser—or with the abuser him- or herself. And the list of feelings goes on. Maybe this disclosure brings up hurtful memories of your own past, making it hard to separate your experience from your child's. Your first concern is, and must be, your child's wellbeing. But what do I do now? This book answers that question.

I have worked with Chris in a professional capacity for almost two decades. She not only is a dedicated and caring professional, but also an effective teacher who shares her knowledge and skills with many other professionals including law enforcement officers, child protection workers, prosecutors and therapists. Those teaching skills come through in this direct, and easy to understand book that gives real examples and specific strategies and advice.

Chris shares from her years as a teacher, therapist, and forensic interviewer of children who have experienced and witnessed abuse. She also recognizes that with hurting children come hurting families. Drawing from her experience, Chris meets you where you are – the unimaginable – and gives you practical information to get to where you so desperately want to be – on the road to healing.

Abuse has impacted your child and you, and you so desperately want to return to a sense of normalcy. Know that while your experience is unique and personal, you are not alone. Take heart! As Chris writes, "abuse does not have to define you." This book gives hope for healing and a pathway to a future beyond the abuse.

Rachel Mitchell, *Maricopa County Career Child Crimes Prosecutor*

INTRODUCTION

My hope for you in reading this book is to have a greater sense of what has happened, what it means for you and your family and provide you with a hopefulness and renewed sense of power to heal and move forward after abuse has been disclosed by your child. I anticipate you will continue to learn and strive to be the parent you want to be for your child. Thus, modeling for your child the type of productive, healthy adult your child has the potential to be. This book aims to provide practical, helpful information for how to deal with the process that can come once a child says he or she has been abused. Each chapter is designed to answer the common questions parents typically have after their child has disclosed being abused. Whether you are a parent, or a professional helping a family, who is dealing with abuse and trauma, the information in this book is intended to help guide you through the emotional process that can ensue. It is also meant to serve as a resource to help better prepare you and your child in navigating the systems (both legal and social) in a more informed and adept manner.

I've worked diligently throughout my professional career to ensure parents and families are armed with the information necessary to face what can be a difficult, sometimes challenging path to healing after abuse occurs. My experience from being in the field of abuse and trauma for over 20 years and working with survivors from various backgrounds, ethnicities and socioeconomic statuses has provided me with the unique ability to provide relevant, practical advice and tools helpful in the healing process when faced with abuse.

I began working with children when I started teaching Spanish to high school students back in the early 90s. I truly loved helping these children, but felt there was so much more I could do to help these children as they revealed to me their problems and the challenges they faced. This drive led me to the decision to head back to college to obtain my master's degree in clinical psychology, something I loved as much as teaching. While taking classes and trying to figure out what I was going to do when I grew up, I needed to take an extracurricular course to satisfy the course hours needed in my program and within my field of study. It just so happened that a new course had been developed that would consist of two full weekends of study with a certain number of hours dedicated to staffing a rape crisis hotline. Now as a college student looking to get as much bang for my buck as possible, this seemed right up my alley. Even though I knew nothing about rape or sexual assault, I was intrigued by the course title, "Rape Crisis." Well, that intrigue suddenly, abruptly changed to one of initial confusion, disbelief and horror! That first weekend **rocked my world**. And I don't mean in an uplifting sort of way. Everything I knew, accepted as reality, in my safe little world was suddenly turned upside down. I began having nightmares, high states of anxiety and yes, a bit of depression after that first full weekend of coursework. I never knew what terror and anguish there could be out there and in such an uncertain world.

With the wonderful support of and mentoring by the amazing women at the Houston Area Women's Center (Cassandra Thomas, Sonia Corrales, Pamela Ellis, and LaDonna Harris), not to mention my college mentor and clinical supervisor (Susan Turell), I was able to reestablish a stronger, more realistic sense of safety and awareness. Understand this was not an overnight process, but as the months and years passed, I was exposed to a unique world of power. The power to help women, men and children regain their voices and their senses of self in a more hopeful, stronger way.

Now my original plan when I went back to college for my master's degree was to work in the state hospital. I loved psychology, studying human behaviors and understanding the human brain and how it functions. I received a terminal master's degree that would allow me to do psychological testing, which was necessary in my plan to help rehabilitate adults who had some form of brain trauma. However, once I discovered this new path, along with the knowledge and skill sets developed through volunteering and later working for the Women's Center, I become adept at providing counseling and supports services for victims. These victims, who became survivors, allowed me the privilege of helping them reintegrate into society in a safer, more informed way. I was very passionate about my work, taking calls on the hotline, meeting survivors at the hospital, and educating the professional community (medical staff, law enforcement, attorneys and the public) on rape, its effect, and how to respond appropriately to it.

Growing up in the South, I led a fairly sheltered life. Now I did not realize that at the time, but the experiences I had early on in my adult career certainly reinforced for me just how sheltered I was. I feel very fortunate to have grown up in a loving, nurturing family. We were not perfect, but we were there for each other, no matter what! I came to realize, that this foundation would provide me with the ability to listen to others' challenges in order to help them find the support they needed.

This eventually led me on a career path to counseling children and their families who were dealing with abuse and the trauma that often accompanies abuse. After moving to Arizona in the late 90s, I found a comparable Center and continued counseling children, their families and adult survivors of abuse. I then transitioned to working primarily with children shortly after I started working for Childhelp Children's Center. Not long after my employment there, I was asked to go into the field of Forensic Interviewing, where I would continue to work with children, but develop a more specialized skill set in communicating with them.

This was where my last mentor, Dr. Wendy Dutton, helped me find my niche to provide the best opportunity for children to not only have a voice, but to have that voice be heard. I've been very blessed in my career to have the privilege as a Dedicated Forensic Interviewer to work with the most highly trained, dedicated professionals. These professionals (law enforcement, child protection workers, medical professionals, counselors, victim advocates, prosecutors, and other attorneys) opened a world of learning to me and provided alongside of me the opportunities to help children and their families from a variety of levels. This has been the most inspirational time for me as it has given me the privilege to help build a safer, more-informed and aware community. From the bottom of my heart, I'm extremely grateful to the individuals and families with whom I've worked – for letting me be a part of their healing journeys and showing me what true strength looks like.

Please remember this book serves as only one resource to help you better understand the dynamics of abuse and the trauma which may accompany it. There are a variety of professionals who have developed websites, published articles, written books and created games to help families better deal with trauma, understand healthy development, and promote healing.

SECTION 1:
MY CHILD JUST SAID SHE WAS
SEXUALLY ABUSED.
NOW WHAT?

CHAPTER 1:
WHAT YOUR CHILD IS THINKING BEFORE SHE OR HE TELLS YOU ABOUT ABUSE

There can be many, many barriers to overcome before deciding to disclose, which can draw out the process for quite a while. It's natural for the abused to begin to question him/herself, especially when the one who committed the abuse is someone loved and trusted. This questioning, or confusion, can play out in a child's head for quite some time before she or he ever decides to try and tell someone what happened, either verbally or behaviorally.

Once the decision to disclose has been made, your child then has to go through the process of choosing whom she will tell.

It's important to note that often times, parents believe they would – or should – be the first person the child chooses to tell. Sometimes this is the case, but more often, it is not.

If your child did not disclose to you first, please know it is not in any way a reflection of your parenting skills or the "closeness" of your relationship with him or her. In fact, the reality could be that your child has so much love and respect for you, that he worries telling you about the abuse would be too devastating and hurtful for you.

Generally, children do not want to upset, disappoint or anger you, the parent or respected adult in their lives. Since revealing abuse can certainly do that, most of us, children and adults, will "test the waters" before actually disclosing. We do this by telling a small portion of information, to see how it's received. This is very common; human beings do not by nature disclose all information, all at once, about anything, much less about abuse.

For example, think for a moment about something that has happened to you or you were a part of in the past. Did you tell your parent about it? Why or why not? If you did, did you disclose everything right away?

Now think of a time when you did something you knew may get you in trouble. Maybe you broke something, you snuck out of the house, or you were someplace you knew you weren't supposed to be. When your parents found out, did you tell them the whole story, from beginning to end, right away? Or did you leave certain parts out? (Maybe you omitted parts like hanging out with someone older, or drinking, or how you were doing something you had been told not to do.) Did you maybe "gloss over" certain pieces of information, praying no one would ask you any further questions about that specific omission?

It's true, you likely didn't want to get in trouble… but that goes hand-in-hand with not wanting to upset your parent.

A similar process occurs with abuse – especially when your child feels as though she did something wrong. The small amount of information your child chooses to initially disclose about the abuse may be what she feels will be believed, least embarrassing, or the least shameful.

From there, based on your child's perception of the reaction she receives to the small bit of information she shares, she will either choose to tell more, change the topic, or stop talking altogether. If she discloses, she may even eventually recant, or take back, all of it. These can be common scenarios.

Again, if your child makes the decision to tell, he has to overcome a number of emotional and psychological barriers and fears in order to do so, like: Will she be believed? What will happen to him? What will happen to the abuser? What will people think of her? Will everyone hate him? Did she do something wrong? Did he deserve this? Is she a bad person? Does this make him a bad person?

These are all important questions, which means your response to the information you receive is pretty important, too.

And this is key: it's not just the response that your child is met with, but your child's perception of that response that determines what she will do next. Understand that your child can interpret responses from others in lots of different ways. And if there is any previous history in your child's life of trauma or abuse, it can greatly affect how your child reads the response, both verbal and nonverbal, she gets after disclosing this abuse.

How we respond to traumatic events, that fight, flight or freeze, can have a major impact on how we read future situations. For example, if you have a child who has been through abusive situations before, this child may freeze at the least sign of anger or aggression. That freeze response can then make your child appear as if he is not listening to you or worse, appear defiant. This can then escalate a parent's frustration and a vicious communication cycle ensues.

Or your child begins to zone out mentally and appears as though she is not even listening to you, the parent, which again can raise levels of frustration and lead to angry responses toward her. Or maybe your child, because of previous abuse experiences, misreads a neutral face and starts to automatically shut down and dissociate. This too can be not only frustrating, but confusing for all involved.

Understanding these potential responses can help improve your communication.

Your response to the "test the waters" information:

Ideally, in the face of potentially devastating revelations, the person receiving the initial "test the waters" information from the child believes and supports the child immediately, actively listening and providing a safe space for the child to disclose, as this is the best and quickest way to start the healing process and ensure a successful recovery.

But don't worry, if that wasn't your initial response. You were in a terribly stressful moment and nothing in these types of situations can be scripted.

Plus, often times, since no one ever really "expects" a child to be abused, parents/adults respond to the initial revelation with questions that result from general shock/disbelief.

Understandable! We so desperately want to regain our sense of power and control that we usually react by instinctually asking questions, and then by placing blame on ourselves.

Let's talk about some of the most common response questions, first.

- Why didn't you tell me?
- Are you sure?
- How did I not know? / How could I have not seen this?
- How could I have brought this person (who hurt my child) into our lives/home? / How could I have trusted this person?
- What could I have done to prevent this? / How could I have let this happen?

ALL of these questions are valid, and if we start to explore the answers with a greater understanding of human behavior and relationships, then we are able to accept the answers. And it's important to process these questions and answers, so you don't inadvertently ask your child questions that could complicate the entire situation. So let's do that now, beginning by breaking them down.

"Why didn't you tell me?"

Many times, this is the first question a parent or adult asks. It's understandable! But it also has unintentional consequences. Let's break this question down for a moment. The first word is "Why?" That makes it sound accusatory, which automatically creates a situation where your child feels the need to defend his or her behaviors, thoughts, or decisions.

To illustrate this further, let's say I ask you why you decided to read this book. As subtle as that may sound, this particular question compels you to give an answer that explains and defends your motivations and thought processes around choosing to read it.

This type of question requires a "cause-and-effect" type answer. However, when it comes to abuse, the cause-and-effect are often rather confusing. When you ask your child this question – *why* they did or did not do something – it is typically because you cannot understand how something like abuse could've happened to your child.

"Are you sure?"

Let's imagine a child begins a verbal "testing the waters" disclosure that is met with a question like, "Are you sure?" Now, this type of response is also quite understandable, right? Especially if you're the parent whose job it is to protect your child. These feelings of protection typically run pretty deep and can surface in a split second. Then there's often an underlying sense of guilt that accompanies that protective mechanism.

It's not necessarily that you do not believe your child or what your child is telling you. It may be the mere fact that what your child is saying is so incredible, you don't want to believe it; you simply cannot wrap your head around it. But that disbelief is distinctly different than not believing or discrediting what a child discloses.

Here's the thing: while understanding your motivation for asking the question may help you understand your initial reaction, it doesn't change what a child may hear/perceive when that question is posed.

To the child, that type of question can imply that he was wrong or misunderstood what happened. This will most likely result in an immediate shut down.

Let's say the child didn't know that what happened to her was abuse, and she begins to say things that lead you to question the certainty of what she is saying. She may then start to sense that what she's saying is "bad" or "wrong," which can also result in her shutting down or recanting, or both.

Once, while interviewing a second-grader, Lily, about her sexual abuse, she described to me how her mommy did not believe her at first. Lily talked about how her mommy kept asking her if it were an accident. She indicated that she then started questioning whether it was an accident, because her aunt's eyes were closed when she was lying next to Lily, rubbing her vagina. But then she saw her aunt's eyes open when Lily moved.

Here, Lily's mom's response to her disclosure was enough to make Lily question her own interpretation of what happened, even more than she already had. This was not intentional on Lily's mom's part, but was the result of her asking for absolute certainty.

It's complicated. Even telling your child – or having your child sense – that what happened was absolutely not okay can "backfire" because it can lead her to believe that she is not okay. Even though you may say something like, "What happened to you was not okay," she might hear, "What happened was not okay and you were involved, so you are not okay." This can be as devastating to a child as much as hearing about abuse can be to a parent.

"How did I not know? / How could I have not seen this?"

This question is borne not only out of shock and disbelief, but also from a sense of powerlessness. You may think "If something like this can happen to me, to my family, then what is safe in this world? Who is safe?" Of course, this can feel daunting.

Let's look at it this way:

Have you ever shared something very personal about yourself with a very dear friend only to have that friend betray your trust and tell someone else what you shared in confidence?

Did you cut off all ties with that friend? If so, how did you treat other friends? Did you make friends after this betrayal? Did you let it affect all your relationships: current and future ones? How did you overcome all of this? While it may have taken you time to get beyond feeling so hurt and betrayed, I'm betting that slowly, step-by-step, you began to reestablish your trust in others and yourself so that your other and new relationships were built on stronger ground.

Or did you talk to that friend and tell her/him how much hurt you felt from this betrayal? Were you able to reestablish your trust in this friend over time, but with clearer, more definite boundaries about your expectations of her/him regarding sharing information about you? If so, I imagine this also took time, but the end result was one of a more secure relationship.

The good news: going through something traumatic can actually help you to rebuild your sense of safety in a more realistic, secure way – one that allows you to feel a truer, greater sense of power. Yes, bad things happen in life. But if we start approaching those life experiences as learning and growing opportunities, then we can start to heal and move forward.

Now I'm not talking about forgiveness at this point. That is a totally different topic. I am talking about not allowing abuse to define who we are, or to determine what path we now have to take. It should not be allowed to affect how we look, act or feel.

"How could I have brought this person (who hurt my child) into

our lives/home? / How could I have trusted this person?"

Understanding the way in which abuse usually occurs may help here. Sexual abuse occurs most commonly in the context of a relationship. Relationships are typically initiated through blood (family) or common interests (friends) and built on trust. This trust is necessary in order to have "intimacy." This trust and intimacy are typically built by the abuser over time, and with those closest to your child, which includes you.

In other words, it's a process, and the abuser establishes a relationship with you *and* your child. This isn't something you necessarily "could or should have seen coming."

"What could I have done to prevent this? / How could I have let this happen?"

It's natural for you to question what you could have done, (and/or what you "should" have done), when you first learn that abuse has occurred. This question deals with a deeper sense of powerlessness and shame.

As the parent, you might feel a range of emotions. All of these are common.

Powerlessness

No one likes (or feels comfortable with) powerlessness. We all want to feel powerful and in control, but sometimes we have to reevaluate and redefine the power we truly have. Doing so allows us to create a more realistic sense of safety and trust. To answer a question of responsibility, we must first establish the roles of those involved in the abuse.

The abused, also known as the primary victim, is the one who has been directly violated.

The secondary victim, anyone who has a relationship with the child that is held "near and dear" to the primary victim's heart, including but not limited to a parent, sibling, grandparent, or friend.

The abuser, the person who created the entire abuse scenario. In defining the abuser's role, we actually answer several of the common questions adults face after hearing abuse has occurred. The abuser is the only person who actually did have the power and control; yet, that is not how we (parent, child, community) typically view it. We question what we did wrong ourselves, when we thought we were in control.

Abusers are manipulators. They manipulate everyone around them, and the environment around them to provide an opportunity for the abuse to occur. Now, I am not saying abusers are necessarily villains, but I am saying they are solely responsible for the abuse.

This can be scary to admit to ourselves, how the abuser held so much power and control, especially if we let it dominate our thoughts, feelings, and behaviors. Understanding it however, can give you true insight into how the abuse, the trust violation and the exploitation occurred.

And this insight will promote your (and your child's) healing.

Shame

In essence, to feel shame, you must believe or feel as though you had a conscious awareness and some semblance of control over something bad that happened. This belief, paired with you believing that you then chose to create, allow, or promote something "bad" or "morally wrong" to occur, gives you a deep sense of regret. In cases of abuse, there was only one person responsible and who was in control: the person who committed the abuse. Those of us on the sidelines, including secondary victims, even if those individuals did not initially believe the disclosure, are not responsible for the abuse.

Holding onto shame tends to cause a person to isolate – to go inward – to choose to NOT share or open up about his or her feelings, negative thoughts, and pain. It often causes us to hide behind an "I'm okay" mask. The problem then becomes the ways in which all of those feelings, negative thoughts, and pain manifest. In his book, The Betrayal Bond, Psychologist Patrick Carnes talks about how shame that results from trauma can manifest as self-deprivation of fun, enjoyment, or pleasure, to over-extending, doing everything for everyone else, as we try to overcompensate for feelings of inadequacy.

Shame holds us back from truly being able to heal, and from beginning to trust again in others, and more importantly, in ourselves.

CHAPTER 2:
THE "BLAME GAME" – SO WHO IS RESPONSIBLE?

Now that we've talked about some of the questions adults/parents commonly ask after a child begins to disclose abuse, let's talk about another process that often occurs: the "blame game."

- "If only I would have…"
- "If only I didn't…"
- "Why did I…"
- "How did I not…?"

Going through this self-questioning process that basically places the blame on yourself, as the adult/parent, is as common as it is false. (Secondary victims commonly go through this process, as well as primary victims.) In fact, if you trusted the abuser, you may even experience self-doubt, distrust of others and in your ability to see people for who they are, and potentially, even self-hatred. Before you go careening down that path, I want you to take a step back and truly look at the overall picture.

Did you listen to your child (even if it took a bit to sink in or wrap your head around it)?

Did you tell yourself (and your child) you are going to do whatever it takes to protect her?

Are you reading this book in hopes of better understanding what happened, how it happened and what to do now?

Then I would say you are taking back your power and doing the best possible thing for your child: healing. (Therapy can also help you, the parent, better process these thoughts and feelings of powerlessness, as well.)

You now have the opportunity to mend with your child. Be honest with him/her. You're human, and you may not have really known how to respond to her at first. Maybe you were in such shock and disbelief that it happened that you weren't able to say exactly what she needed to hear. It is okay to let your child know you are not perfect, and you do make mistakes, but that you acknowledge that mistake and won't repeat it.

All that said, this is more than a difficult situation: it gets to be downright precarious. Even if the child's disclosure of abuse is met with a warm, protective and understanding response, there can still be unintentional fallout, which can occur through the natural course of the investigation, or with life in general after the secret of abuse is revealed.

So what IS the "right" response?

All you really have to do is allow your child to provide you with his experience. In other words, you provide the safe space, and listen.

That's ALL you have to do at this stage, and then you can better prepare yourself for "the fallout".

Once your child "lets the cat out of the bag" so to speak, expect what some call the fallout. This refers to all of the changes that can result once abuse has been disclosed.

Why do I say to expect and prepare for it? Because it's inevitable. Life IS different now. You are different. Your child is different. The family is different. Maybe you have instantly become a single-income family. Maybe you have to move out of your house after losing your job, because you are no longer as productive as you were. Maybe you have lost relationships. Those friends and family who choose not to support you, even after dealing with their own disbelief, are not likely to change even if you or your child try to minimize the abuse or make things seem like they were before.

There are numerous ways your life can be disrupted in the face of abuse, but please know that it does not have to be all doom and gloom! As I mentioned above, you now have the opportunity to rebuild. You will find people who will support you and your child, and help you in that rebuilding process. In fact, some of your relationships – and some of the child's relationships – will actually become stronger, built on more stable ground.

CHAPTER 3:
THE WAYS YOUR CHILD MAY DISCLOSE

Let's talk now about the disclosure itself, which is often a process that happens over time, and in accordance with environmental, psychological and emotional factors. While it is not an easy process, it could be something that gives the child a sense of power and better understanding of what happened and where to go next, when the disclosure is met with a consistent and appropriate response.

Children may choose to purposefully disclose abuse to someone whom they feel will listen to them, believe them and comfort them. There is no set pattern of how long the abuse has occurred or what kind of abuse it was that determines when a child may purposefully disclose. What we do know is that the closer the relationship between the abused and the abuser, the harder it is to disclose.

Children may also be prompted to disclose abuse. This can happen when someone asks the child if something, like abuse, has happened. Realize that a prompted disclosure still results in the same mental process as a purposeful disclosure: the child still has to make decisions about what to tell and how much to tell, if anything. The above-referenced factors can still impact this type of disclosure as well.

Now some children do not intend to disclose abuse, but maybe through the course of play, a typical conversation about ordinary things, or even a heated argument may mention or blurt out an abusive act. This accidental disclosure, like the purposeful and prompted disclosures, can also be affected by the response your child receives – and his perception of it – which again can determine what happens next. For example, if your child has no idea that what he has disclosed was something that was not supposed to happen, and you react in a way that reflects how wrong it is, he may negatively read your facial or body cues, or your tone of voice, and start to shut down.

Let's explore this a bit more. The scientific community is now beginning to better understand how early trauma affects the brain and its development. Basically, there is a "rewiring" of the brain that occurs with early trauma and childhood abuse. Now, this does NOT mean that your child will be cognitively impaired or that there is something wrong with your child's brain because of the abuse. What it can mean is that children may tend to over-read nonverbal cues, such as a furrowed brow. For example, your furrowed brow may reflect confusion or even disbelief that something like this could happen to your child, but your child may read that furrowed brow as a reflection of anger.

Now, imagine telling someone about something that happened to you, like abuse, which can make you feel embarrassed, scared, and/or ashamed, only to be met with what you feel (and fear) is anger or an implied accusation of lying.

Communication – verbal and nonverbal – can be difficult, if not downright tricky, at times!

Consider this:

Have you ever been talking to your partner about something, and you're saying one thing, but your partner is hearing something else completely? To complicate it further, you continue communicating without even realizing a disconnect is occurring until later, well into the discussion, when maybe a disagreement ensues.

If emotions are high, like they are in a heated argument, it will be more difficult to truly begin the dialogue again, during which you are patiently listening to your partner's response before forming your own. However, once things cool off, you are much better equipped to be able to listen, check your understanding/perception of what was actually said, and then respond calmly.

As previously mentioned, the process of communication is not always an easy obstacle for adults to overcome. It's even more difficult for children.

So when something like trauma occurs early on in our lives, and our brain has learned to accommodate and cope with what happened (by rewiring itself), the rewired brain can't just suddenly go back to the way it was (before the abuse). So say you are having a discussion with a friend, who is also your coworker. Now during a discussion at work, you are becoming upset as she is talking about what you did on a project because you feel as though your friend is being critical of something you did. In reality however, your friend is simply commenting on what you had done, but there was something in her tone and maybe some expression you saw on her face that led you to feel as though she were being critical of you. When questioned about this, you may try to deny your hurt feelings and simply not ask for clarification. However, this can then lead to misunderstandings and difficulty relating to others.

This over-reading or misreading can be quite common, but takes some time if you are to change this. You may get a little more savvy about how to disguise your misreadings as you get older and more indoctrinated into societal norms, but your underlying initial, automatic response (misreading or overreading) is still there. Learning how to overcome this response and incorporate skills which allow for a more adept way of reading emotions and checking your understanding of what was said (rewiring) will prevent you from jumping to incorrect conclusions. It does not mean this rewired brain is unintelligent or incapable. Quite the contrary, it is powerfully adaptive, and will figure out other ways to accomplish learning on how to better communicate and be more confident in your relationships.

Consider adults who have suffered brain injuries. While the brain may lose some functioning, it rewires a "workaround" so that we are able to continue to function and be productive. Research has long demonstrated how children and animals do this, as well. For example, have you ever "inherited" a dog, who was fearful of something, like men or kids or women wearing heels? Your dog does not intentionally dislike these individuals, but because of early traumatic life experiences, your dog now automatically has a fearful (possibly aggressive) reaction when experiencing that particular trigger. With some behavior training, the brain can reprogram its response to these triggers so that it is one of understanding instead of fear or aggression. This is exactly how therapy helps abused children learn how to respond to environmental stimuli that can trigger fear, anger, or any number of reactions when encountered.

Nonverbal Disclosure

Now some children will provide nonverbal cues about the abuse, and truly feel they have told someone about what happened. The difficulty is you don't typically recognize these nonverbal cues at the time, it's usually only in hindsight that you start putting all the pieces together and realize your child was trying to tell us about the abuse. For your child, the really difficult part here is that, if she feels like she has told and the abuse continues, she may begin to feel like it's pointless to do anything further, because no one will intervene on her behalf. This can lead to a sense of learned helplessness where your child may simply realize there is no way out of an abusive situation so she figures out other ways to cope with what is happening to her.

What might nonverbal cues look like? Again, you may not be aware of what is going on for your child in the exact moment, but you may see some behaviors that are not typical for your child. You may notice your child being more clingy and not wanting you to leave his side. This can occur when it's just the two of you or when others are around, including people with whom the child has a close relationship. You may notice behavioral outbursts, such as crying fits or tantrums. Or you may see regressive behaviors, like your child acting younger than her chronological age. You may also notice your child's attitude or personality are different such as, he gets upset easier over minor things or is more rebellious towards you, only to then turn around and be more clingy towards you.

If a child has demonstrated any of the above, this does not necessarily mean she is being abused; only that there is something causing your child to have a difficult time dealing with something and a discussion with your child needs to follow.

CHAPTER 4:
THE TIMING OF TELLING YOU

Many times, as adults, we question why it might take a child so long to disclose what has happened.

I invite you to think of it this way:

Throughout the course of life, when things that are confusing, embarrassing, negative, or shameful occur, reluctance in discussing them is something everyone experiences, especially children.

Children who suffer abuse and feel as though they have no real power or voice find various ways to not have to talk about what happened: sometimes forever, and sometimes just until they are sure it's safe, knowing they will be believed, or at the very least, heard without judgment.

Kids naturally look to parents to determine whether or not people, places, events, etc. are safe. When you try to convince, cajole or coerce your child into thinking that things are okay, while you yourself are feeling nervous, anxious, or even scared, it transfers to your child.

A similar process can occur when a parent is afraid of certain insects or animals. Say you grew up with a fear of dogs. Now once you grow up and have a child, that fear does not magically go away. Your relationship with your child is so close that your innate fear any time you are faced with a dog's presence is modeled and most often nonverbally expressed in front of your child. Thus, being your child's greatest "learning tool", that fear can be transferred to your child, who now may also have an automatic fear of dogs. A dog has never bitten, growled, or maybe even barked at your child, but after having witnessed or experienced your anxiety and fear of dogs your child now unconsciously believes dogs are to be feared and avoided.

Children give a variety of reasons for not telling right away, or sooner than we hope. Although they usually don't initially understand the full extent of what happened, just feeling that something isn't right makes them question what to do about it.

During an interview with an 11-year-old girl, Lisa, she described how confused she was over all the feelings she had about her older brother repeatedly sexually abusing her for years. Lisa described feeling so scared initially, but completely trusting her brother because he was the oldest and used to look out for her. Lisa explained how she eventually not only learned how to tell when the abuse was going to happen, but also how to begin to prepare for it. When I asked Lisa how she knew something was going to happen with her older brother, she replied that it would start with him telling her to wear her ladybug pajamas.

She explained, "That's how I knew what he wanted because my ladybug pajamas were kind of loose and he could get his hand under my clothes. I got so used to it, I just started taking them off before I went to sleep because I knew what was going to happen. By then, I think I must've liked it because I took off my clothes and would lie there waiting for him."

This description of Lisa's thoughts and feelings about the abuse, including the preparation, is not uncommon for children who have been chronically abused. This child learned how to survive. She learned how to cope with a situation that not only didn't make sense, but that also violated a sacred trust among those she loved the most: her family. What Lisa did not understand, beyond the 'WHY did this happen,' is the fact that she was so well-groomed by her abuser, she knew the routine so well – that she used that knowledge as one of the only ways she had to regain some semblance of power over the situation.

Another child, Jack, a 10-year-old boy who was sexually abused by his dad over a period of years, described how he and his dad used to have "Boy Talk Time." Jack explained how in the beginning, when he was seven or eight years old, it was cool because his sisters weren't there and he had his dad all to himself. Jack also described how, at first, he thought it was a little weird, but kind of neat too that his dad would let him look at some pictures of naked ladies on his phone. His dad would then talk to him over the next several months about what to do with girls, and what he could expect the girls to do to him. Jack described how some weeks later, he basically froze the first time his dad "did it."

During the interview, it took Jack quite some time to describe what "it" was, but he eventually revealed that his father put his mouth on Jack's penis and then put his penis in Jack's butt. Jack also reported that his father told him he was doing it to let him know what it felt like, and that there was nothing wrong with a father showing his son. Jack talked about being so confused by his father's actions, knowing too that his mom would not approve of him having looked at porn. Jack talked about how his father had even told him one time that Jack should say something if he did not like what he (his father) was doing, but that Jack did not know what to say because this was his father… and Jack was afraid of what his mother would say, feel or think.

In fact, he was so confused by all of it that he didn't know what to do, other than to do nothing at all.

For Jack, his was a prompted disclosure that came after a school presentation on Good, Bad and Secret Touches, where Jack finally learned his father's behaviors were not okay and to trust his feelings about what happened. What Jack did not understand then was that his father's behaviors were actually preparing him for the intended abuse his father had planned for him. This was a slow eroding of Jack's resistance to behaviors that would normally not be "okay" for Jack to experience. Jack did not like it, but his father was able to convince him (groom him) in a way that made Jack question himself, not his father, and so the abuse continued.

Now that we've covered the different types of disclosures, and your reaction, what do you actually DO after a child has told you he's been abused? That's what we're covering next.

SECTION 2:
NOW THAT I KNOW ABOUT THE ABUSE… WHAT COMES NEXT?

CHAPTER 5:
THE POST-DISCLOSURE PROCESS

When a child tells you she has been abused, it can be upsetting, unsettling, and painful for everyone involved.

In fact, it can be so painful, we fall into immediate denial.

Denial has many faces. It's more than, "I can't believe this," or "I won't believe this."

When we come across something that goes against what we *know*, what we *believe*, or what we *recognize*, and it's contradictory to our world value, the natural inclination is to reject it, discredit it and *disbelieve* it. Otherwise, our world is not safe, and it's certainly not comfortable.

Have you ever been laid off or fired? Have you ever had someone close to you suddenly die? I imagine these events brought up similar feelings as those we experience as a result of an abuse disclosure, and you probably had to find a way to deal with the initial shock. You also had to eventually cope with what happened.

Denial can play a very necessary role for us at times. It helps us get through tough, painful events. As long as you can push whatever it is back, push it away, you don't have to deal with it, right?

Sometimes, the initial numbness we feel as a result of shock is exactly what helps us be capable of dealing with the immediacy of the event. Once that numbness wears off though, we are left with other ways to try and comprehend what happened, and cope with what happened. One of those other ways is absolutely through denial. When we are in denial, we are able to continue on in our "normal" life because it provides for us a false sense of safety and security. We are able to function.

The problem is that sense of normalcy will crumble, and then, we're left with the actual reality of the hurt, disbelief, shame, and embarrassment – everything we were trying to avoid feeling while in denial. To make matters worse, it tends to bring any insecurities you have to the surface in an even more painful way. At some point, you'll find yourself exhausted, because you are constantly questioning everything: every decision, every conversation, every motivation behind everyone's behaviors. This is all because being in denial keeps us from dealing effectively with reality, and more importantly, from healing from that hurtful, unbelievable, shameful and embarrassing event.

When you, the parent/adult, are faced with the reality of abuse, going into denial – not dealing with it or believing it – might feel like the best way for you to move on, but really, it will just keep you stuck, prolonging the pain and suffering, as you find yourself forever questioning, wondering what is/was real, who people truly are, their motives, and so forth. And while denial does serve a purpose (as described above), it also creates negative long-term effects that can lead to unsuccessful and unhappy relationships and interactions.

Clearly, denial is a powerful mechanism that can also skew our take on what we witness. Be careful to make sure it doesn't affect your ability to provide your child the best opportunity to be heard.

Remember, all you have to do is allow your child to provide you with his experience.

In order to minimize the traumatic effect an initial disclosure may have on your child, be sure to do your best to listen attentively and without judgment. You know your child, and your child knows you, so when he starts to tell you about abuse and it seems so unbelievable to you that this could have even happened, please don't interrupt him, but let him talk and be sure he knows you are glad he told you. You can deal with your disbelief later.

CHAPTER 6:
PARENTAL DOS AND DON'TS

Resist the urge to ask your child tons of questions in the exact moment of his disclosure, before the official investigation from law enforcement or child protection is underway. The questions you ask may not be the "right" questions that will bring you the information you are seeking and may affect the way your child discloses his experience of what happened to him.

This is why it is SO important to only ask four questions:
- What happened?
- Who did it?
- Where were you when this happened?
- When did this happen? *(Used mainly to determine the need for medical attention.)*

Please allow the specially-trained professionals (law enforcement, child protection workers, and dedicated forensic interviewers) to get at the meaning and context, of the disclosure. Doing so ensures that everyone will gain a better understanding of what happened and obtain the most knowledge possible.

Do not ask the child to demonstrate what happened to him or her on your body, his or her own body, or by using dolls. The instinct to want to fully grasp what your child has just told you is understandable, but often times, asking for a demonstration of any kind can lead to more confusion on your part, as well as more apprehension on your child's part.

Resist the urge to record your child's statement. With easy access to computers, mobile devices, phones, tablets, etc., you may think it is a good idea to record your child telling you what happened. Maybe you want to avoid misconstruing what your child actually said, or maybe you intend to use it as "proof" of what your child disclosed. However, think of it this way: Would YOU want something that was confusing, painful, hurtful, shameful, and/or embarrassing to be recorded for posterity? You may think this can be used in court as proof, but unlike in court scenes you may see on television, the reality is that we are typically not allowed to bring in these items and they are of little, if any, evidentiary value.

The reason we do not typically record counseling sessions is that, for healing to take place, a lot of hard, sometimes very painful work must occur. Remember that counseling is private and confidential (with very few exceptions: like in cases of harm to oneself or harm to others) because without that confidentiality, there would not be a sense of emotional safety or allowing yourself to be vulnerable. Would you really want to go back and watch/listen to yourself talking about your pain, feeling that pain over and over again? Would it serve a purpose in your healing?

History is a great learning tool, but we don't necessarily need to repeat it to overcome or to heal from abuse.

Never have your child confront the person he is accusing of abuse. There is absolutely no purpose in you doing this at any time after a child has made an abuse disclosure. In fact, when an adult does choose this course of action, it is often to allay his or her *own* initial fears and has absolutely no benefit to your child. It will likely make him either recant what he said or start to just shut down and not say anything more. (Ever.)

Rest assured there will be a time and place later for this confrontation, but it's NOT immediately after your child discloses. (If this is something that's already happened, and you did choose to have the child confront the abuser, it's important to talk to him now and let him know you made a mistake. Reassure him that you won't make him do it again.)

In one of my interviews of a 10-year-old boy's mom, Luisa, she talked about how, after her son Angel told her how his cousin, Gus, was touching Angel's penis with his hand, she brought him over to Gus' house so Angel could repeat this disclosure to his uncle Daniel. Luisa described how her son literally recoiled and hid behind her when she began telling Daniel all that Angel had disclosed to her. She also recounted how Daniel immediately started yelling at her, after Gus strongly denied anything "inappropriate" happening.

Even worse, Luisa reported that, as she told Daniel that Gus had touched Angel's penis with his hand, Angel begged her to stop, and then ran back home.

For Luisa, this added to her confusion. She questioned even more if the abuse happened because Angel would not confront Gus.

When I interviewed Angel, he was able to talk openly about "safe" subjects, like the things he enjoyed doing, and school, but when it came to the point in the interview where I invited him to talk about what happened, he completely shut down.

I focused on helping Angel feel more comfortable in the interview again, and afterward, brought up the topic again. Instead of shutting down again, this time, he recanted. He said nothing happened, and claimed to have a really hard time remembering things – even the accused's name and what had happened exactly.

Clearly, this was Angel's way of not having to discuss what was already feeling to him like a "no-win" situation.

Sophia, an 11-year-old girl who had a very close relationship with both of her grandparents (she explained how they were like second parents), went through a similar confrontation. She talked through tears about how her grandmother, upon hearing Sophia's disclosure of how her grandfather forced her to touch his penis, made Sophia tell her grandfather what she had disclosed to her grandmother. It took quite some time (and many tissues) in the interview before Sophia stopped crying, took some deep breaths, composed herself, and was able to talk again about what had happened.

As Sophia expressed how much shame and embarrassment she felt, she also talked about how she had not planned to tell her parents about the abuse because she just wanted to forget about it. However, her grandmother had already called her mother and told her what Sophia had disclosed. Sophia explained that when her mother arrived to pick her up, her grandmother yelled at her mother about how Sophia was a liar and trouble-maker, and was therefore never allowed back to their house again.

Sophia shared how she had never felt as alone and scared in her life as she had in that moment.

She also explained how she had tried to convince her mother, in front of her grandparents, that it was all a mistake and she was just confused about what happened. It was not until her mother and father talked to her at home, when they told her they believed her and knew it was not her fault that Sophia was able to admit the full truth of what happened.

For both Angel and Sophia, there was not only a violation of trust, but also a complete disruption of their secure family attachment and support system. It became too much for Angel and Sophia to deal with, so they desperately wanted to take everything back – for things to "just be normal" again. While this is of course totally understandable, it's also impossible.

For Angel, the effect of the confrontation was one of fear and then recantation. No one, other than Angel, may ever know what exactly happened. It will depend upon how much support and understanding he receives going forward. Now that Luisa fully understands how the confrontation made everything even harder on Angel, she will be continuing his therapy as she begins to repair her relationship with Angel.

For Sophia, the effect of the confrontation was also to initially shut down and then recant, but once her parents removed her from the confrontational situation and told her they believed her, she was able to talk about what happened.

That longing for things to go back to the way they were, the familiar, is normal, but it is not possible.

Do not ask or insist your child tell someone else (friend, family member, etc.) to see if his story changes from what he told you. While you may think doing so will determine whether or not he is telling the truth about being abused, it does nothing of the sort.

Often times, when we talk about an event we have experienced, the details we provide can change slightly depending on how many times we've talked about it, to whom we've talked about it, and where we've talked about it. This is the same with adults and children, alike, and is not an indicator of truth versus lies.

Why do the details change?

Well, have you ever played the telephone game, where a simple message turns out to be something completely different and convoluted when whispered from one person to the next, to the next, and to the next?

What happened to the message once it got to the last person?

It was nearly unrecognizable, wasn't it? Totally different than how it started. And everyone was surprised at how drastically the message changed – even when every single participant was careful to repeat what they heard word-for-word to the next person in line.

So how is it possible for a simple message to not only be completely misstated, but also misunderstood throughout such a seemingly simple communication game?

Everyone brings to a conversation her or his own perceptions that are based off of individual life experiences. Plus, we often forget as adults the process in which language develops. When we are young, we utilize language that is very concrete, literal, and simple. It is not until we start getting older, around the preteen phase, that our brains allow us to better understand more abstract concepts that we can express in our language.

In addition, your child may not attribute the same social norms to his language as you would. For example, one little boy described how during the abuse he suffered, his grandpa would "look" at him. His mother tried to figure out exactly how his grandpa would look at him through asking a series of questions. However, what she did not take into account, and what we later learned, was that the boy was being very concrete and literal in his language. While she was asking him questions about the type of look he received from his grandfather, all he would do is repeat that his grandfather "looked" at him. So while his mother was asking if his grandfather had been giving him a mean, angry, or intimidating type of look, the boy was simply stating that his grandfather was looking specifically at his private part, as opposed to any other body part. (See what I mean when I say "literal and concrete"?)

This is just one example of how communication can go awry with children. This communication pitfall can happen at any time when children and adults are talking, regardless of the type of relationship between the child and adult (parent, teacher, coach, police officer, child protection worker, etc.).

Now imagine the message as something embarrassing, scary, or downright incomprehensible.

Reiterating the circumstances around a traumatic event is hard enough to do once. A variance in detail is to be expected, especially when considering the language differences between children and adults. (Keep this in mind if you also find some elements of your child's disclosure to be so incredible that you think there is no way it could possibly be true. It could be some sort of communication issue like the above.)

CHAPTER 7:
THE PROCESS OF INVESTIGATING
THE ABUSE

A formal investigation by the proper authorities needs to be conducted, for your child's sake and for the sake of any other child the abuser might come into contact with. You need to obtain the following information *if* your child has not already provided it:

- What happened?
- Who did it?
- Where were you when this happened?
- When did this happen? *(Used mainly to determine the need for medical attention.)*

This is the information you will need to provide in order to open an investigation with law enforcement and/or a child protection agency. The investigator assigned to your case will guide you through what happens from there.

It's likely you'll have already gotten the "what" and probably the "who" from your child's initial outcry and/or disclosure, but if not, be sure to ask.

The "where" is important when it comes to something like sexual abuse, which you are required by law to report to law enforcement. (If it is sexual abuse that has occurred with someone in the child's home, you will also need to call Child Protective Services.) You'll need to contact the law enforcement agency in the area in which the abuse occurred.

For example, let's say you live in Phoenix, Arizona, but your child disclosed he was abused while visiting a relative in another location, say Lake Charles, Louisiana. Since the crime occurred in Lake Charles, you'd need to file a police report with the Lake Charles Police Department. A quick note here: Law enforcement agencies work together to assist victims of crime, so in the situation above, if you live in Phoenix, you will not necessarily be required to drive to the Lake Charles Police Department to be interviewed. Usually, the Lake Charles Police Department would contact your local police department and ask them to assist with the investigation, As a result, you and your child would likely be interviewed locally. The same principle applies if the abuse occurred in any different location (city, county, parish or state) within the United States.

You will need the "when" to help investigative professionals better determine whether your child needs immediate medical care. (This does not refer to how many times abuse may have occurred or the specific dates and times of each incident. So please do not ask your child this. It is only in reference to the most recent occurrence.)

If the most recent occurrence falls into a specific time frame, certain medical exams can be ordered that may provide evidence in the case (they are also sometimes covered financially within the context of a police investigation and therefore cost the parent/adult no out-of-pocket expense). However, a medical exam is not only helpful in an investigation. It can also help your child process some of the aftermath of abuse related to his body. One of the effects of abuse can be that children feel as though their bodies are bad, weird, disgusting, or just plain different. The medical exam can help a child understand that his body is normal, after abuse has occurred.

After law enforcement has been contacted and an investigation has begun, you can expect to meet a variety of professionals dedicated to helping you and your child through this difficult time. Most likely, you'll give your initial statement to a patrol officer, who will then pass along your information to a Detective, who will be responsible for gathering all the facts of the case, beginning with your child's statement.

Next, you and your child will likely be asked to go to an "Advocacy Center." These are facilities designed with your – and your child's – comfort in mind. These Centers typically have a waiting area, a play area for the children, and safe, comfortable offices where various interviews take place. A common practice is for the interviewer to first meet with you: the parent, guardian, adult expert on your child. You will be asked a series of questions about your child, his abilities and experiences, and your knowledge of what has been disclosed thus far.

Note: If the abuser is a family member living in your home, or someone with routine, present contact with your child, a Child Protection Agency may become involved. A child safety specialist is someone who is specially trained to work with children and families dealing with abuse and neglect issues. Depending on who is involved in the abuse of your child, the child safety specialist and law enforcement agencies are mandated to work together with the family to ensure your child's safety, while also providing your family with necessary resources.

From here, the child is interviewed.

Considering how your child has already had to overcome numerous hurdles just to get to the point of telling you about the abuse, it's natural to feel concerned about how he might feel anxious, nervous, or even reluctant to talk about it more, especially to a stranger. Here's some good news: more often than not, it's actually easier for a child to make fuller disclosures to "strangers" like police, child safety specialists, or dedicated forensic interviewers.

Here's the thing: There is really no risk to the child when talking to one of these professionals, because the child won't typically see that person on a daily basis. Whereas with you, there is BIG risk. In fact, their whole world can potentially turn upside down when they disclose abuse to someone close to them. Their sense of safety can be thrown off completely. Their greatest fears – not being believed, getting in trouble, their parents being mad at them – can come true in that one, single moment.

Children actually find it easier to talk to a professional as opposed to you about these types of things also as a result of their fear, embarrassment, shame, and most importantly, because of their reluctance to disappoint you.

But with a "stranger," it's just not the same. Your child usually feels "safer."

And not only does a child need to feel safe and comfortable while talking about abuse, but the professional must earn the child's trust. This is not accomplished by your trying to convince your child to go talk to this professional about the abuse – to trust him or her, in an effort to comfort her. The best thing you can do for your child is to remain as calm as possible, knowing that your mere presence is all the confidence and support your child needs in that moment. It will not help to hug, kiss, and repeatedly tell your child how much you love her or how brave she is immediately before the interview. In fact, it could have an adverse effect: your child might begin taking inadvertent cues from you, the kind that tell her something bad, scary, untrustworthy, or painful is about to happen. That could cause your child to shut down before the interviewer even gets the chance to talk to her.

Remember that it's natural for you to be frightened, worried, and/or concerned about what your child may say or how your child might do in the interview, but those are *your* feelings – your child may not be necessarily feeling any of it. You as the parent or trusted adult have an awesome power and ability to instill trust and confidence in your child, just by being a calm, supportive presence – which provides your child a better opportunity to express his experience of the abuse.

Again, the child's sense of trust with the professional who interviews him must be developed through the professional's respect for and genuine interest in the child, his beliefs, values, and knowledge. As you are the expert on your child, sharing your knowledge and expertise with these professionals can go a long way in helping them build that trust with your child.

Children learn by example – most specifically, your example. If you allow yourself to relax, ask questions that help you better understand the process you're going through, and talk about your concerns and fears, it will make a difference in your feelings about the abuse, the investigation, and life after the disclosure. This will in turn affect how the child does the same. Even while outside of your physical presence, your child will feel your emotional state, so again, do your best to remain calm and relaxed.

Dedicated professionals with training in child development, trauma, and abuse understand that the best way for your child's voice to be heard is through a good forensic interview. The interviews are not typical in regard to the "normal" way adults talk to children. In fact, a forensic interview is a specialized method used to obtain the most information possible from your child, without leading or suggesting to your child what happened.

A forensic interviewer is specially trained to talk to children. His or her only job is to be a neutral fact-finder. Knowledge about your child's developmental abilities, communication skills, attention span, and processing abilities are what allow a forensic interviewer to accomplish her job.

She will not force your child to talk, or to say anything; however, every opportunity for a safe environment within which to discuss what happened will be provided. It is not like therapy, where your child may play to express feelings and thoughts about what happened. It is a gentle, neutral conversation about the abuse-related event(s).

The forensic interview is typically conducted one-on-one with the child and a forensic interviewer while the adult/parent waits in another room. During this time, you may talk to other allied professionals, such as a victim advocate, a crisis specialist, or even a counselor. These professionals help with some of the emotional fallout that can happen after abuse. They have expertise and knowledge regarding how to help, and which community resources would be the best fit for you and your family. Meeting with these professionals can allow you time to vent, express your fears, worries, concerns, or even confusion over what happened.

Our greatest fear, the fear of the unknown, can be gently eroded during this process.

Next, we'll cover what to expect after the investigation is officially underway.

CHAPTER 8:
YOUR RESPONSIBILITIES AS A PARENT

A mandated reporter is someone who is responsible (by law) to report any abuse of a child. This includes professionals such as teachers, day care workers, clergy, law enforcement, counselors, etc. But it also includes you the parent. Not only is this important legally, but also for your child to be able to develop a sense of security and stability.

Please remember the four questions you will need to ask (or already have answered from your child's initial abuse disclosure):

- What happened?
- Who did it?
- Where were you when this happened?
- When did this happen? (*Used mainly to determine the need for medical attention.*)

Once you have the answers to your questions, you will need to contact the police department in the city where the abuse happened. (Even if that is not where you live.) A great online resource for locating any law enforcement agency in the United States is www.policeone.com. On this website you can select the state from a drop-down menu and then use the next drop-down menu to select the type of agency by scrolling down their list to find either the police department or sheriff's department.

If the abuse involves someone who is also responsible for the care and custody of your child (parent, stepparent, grandparent, other relatives or close family friends), you will need to contact Child Protective Services (or the agency responsible for ensuring children's safety) too. They have a hotline where you can choose to remain anonymous.

Please keep in mind this systemic response, whether from law enforcement, child protection services or both, or even later down the line in the courts, is not going to be like what you may have seen on television from shows such as CSI, Law & Order and the like. The real life systems are going to take longer and require steps to be taken in a particular order to ensure justice is served and the community is safe.

SECTION 3:
THE AFTERMATH OF DISCLOSURE

CHAPTER 9:
WILL MY CHILD BE SCARRED
FOR LIFE?

As parents, guardians, or trusted adults, we want to protect our children. After abuse, we are often faced with a ton of additional questions as we worry about the long-term effects of abuse.

At this point, it's common to wonder things like:
- What happens next, after the investigation?
- Should I talk to my child about this, or will it just make all the bad memories continuously resurface?
- Will he/she forget about what happened?
- Will my child be scarred for life?

These are all valid questions, but let me ask you a few:

First, I want you to go back into your memory banks and think about a time you felt very embarrassed or ashamed over something that happened in your childhood.

- Did you remember it?
- How are your feelings about it now? Are they different than they were then?
- Did you remember the event in great detail, or just the general gist of what happened?

You probably remember the gist of what happened, with maybe a few details you can recall more clearly than others. That's because emotions are tied to our memories, which sometimes allow us to better remember certain things than others. Or maybe you remember the time you peed your pants at school, and everyone made fun of you, or the teacher brought the class' attention to it, which made you feel even more embarrassed or ashamed. Or maybe you remember the feeling of your mom, dad, or grandparent holding and rocking you when something scared or upset you. You may not remember what it was that actually upset you, but you remember the safety and comfort you felt in your mother's, father's, or grandparent's arms. Whatever the reason – memories and the feelings attached to them – can come up when we least expect it. They can also be triggered by a smell, sound, or sight.

Perhaps you were not be able to pull up a memory at all just now, because it blends into all the other memories.

Let's talk for a moment about the brain.

Our brain is designed to be incredibly efficient. The memories we obtain for routine events (things you do frequently) are easily compiled into one general memory.

If I were to ask you what you did ten weeks ago today, you would probably be able to tell me about your general routine on that day. For example, let's say the day we are talking about is a Sunday, and you know that Sundays are your days to catch up on chores before starting the work and school week. You would probably be able to describe your chore routine, but you may not be able to give much specific detail about that particular Sunday, ten weeks ago.

Now, let's say something specific and memorable happened ten weeks ago, like you had a baby. Because you know your baby is ten weeks old this Sunday, you would be able to give me more information and detail about the day your baby was born than you could about a "normal, routine" Sunday. The baby memory is attached to a unique event, which allows you to pull up more rich detail about that day ten Sundays ago.

I like to think of our brains as having a distinctive filing system in which memories are stored. Now, that does not mean you have every memory nicely organized in alphabetical order, readily available and at your disposal. It also does not mean that your brain will store the details of an event the same way a child's brain will. The filing system is based on your unique knowledge and experiences, and how important (salient) the event was to you. Your brain will choose which memories to keep, and where. The way in which you retrieve the memory of a particular event varies depending on its salience to you and the emotions tied to it.

There are some memories of traumatic or painful events that come back up for us no matter how hard we try to push them down or away, or what we do to try and avoid them. That's likely because we haven't emotionally dealt with or processed them effectively yet. Memories for traumatic or upsetting events are best dealt with by having a positive, nurturing, support system, accomplished with counseling and with your trusted loved ones and friends. Having a better understanding of the feelings you have tied to those memories and their significance to you (what they mean to you/about you) will allow you to more easily work with these memories. Navigating the potential tough times ahead while processing things like abuse, not to mention helping your child along the way, can be improved by dealing with these memories as they come up.

Memories, what our brain chooses to keep and forget, and how we file them, all differ based on our perceptions of the events in our lives. That's why simply saying your child will forget in time, or that your child will always remember every detail of the abuse is far from accurate.

There are many things that can affect our memories, in addition to the emotions attached to them. The responses we receive from others, the understanding of what happened, and what we find to be most relevant or personally salient also affect what we choose to remember and how we remember it. That's why your child will remember things in one way now, and as she learns more about social norms and the world around her, those memories may be altered.

So let's say your three-year-old was sexually abused by your babysitter, and when she disclosed what happened, it sounded to you as if she wasn't really bothered by it. Your child may mention it again later on, but eventually, she stops bringing it up at all. One day, out of the blue it seems, she says something about it again. Only now it's months (or longer) down the line. It's surprising to you because your child never said anything more for such a long time.

There could be any number of things that prompted your child's recollection of the memory. A smell, a sound, the feel of something, or a certain statement could have brought that memory to the forefront of her mind.

This is not to say that children can't forget abusive acts, or that those memories are forever destined to sit right at the top of the memory banks. Our brain, being a rather efficient mechanism, has a way of pulling things up when it's necessary... sometimes when we least expect it... and sometimes when we're actually ready to deal with them.

How we deal with those memories when they surface and where we try to put them (pushed all the way back to the dark corners of our brains versus a readily-accessible file) can determine the effect it has on our behaviors. Bottom line: If we don't deal with the emotions and thoughts at the time of the abuse or shortly thereafter, it can come out sideways, through our behaviors, and kids are no exception.

Even if your child does not talk about what happened or does not want to talk about it, you may start to see behaviors that are out of character for her. For example, you may start to notice her acting younger than her actual age or using baby talk. While this may be extremely frustrating to you, what you need to understand is that she is trying to feel safer, and more comfortable talking to you as she may be dealing with feelings of confusion, distrust, and anxiety.

While talking to the parents of a 7-year-old girl, Renee, about having witnessed any changes in Renee's behaviors recently, her mother Janelle talked about Renee acting like a dog for the past year. She shared how Renee would act that way every time she or Renee's father, Leslie, would ask Renee a question. Janelle stated that the behavior seemed to have gotten worse since Renee disclosed abuse by her brother. Leslie described how Renee would bark at them, pant, and go in circles on her knees while discussing things like Renee's chores or homework, which weren't completed. They explained how odd these behaviors seemed to them, like

Renee was acting like a younger child living in a pretend world. They also talked about how Renee seemed to be clingier. They felt like they couldn't do anything without her being right by them. She also "pitched a fit" whenever they left her with someone else. Leslie said they were getting calls from her teacher at school about this dog-like behavior happening during homework assignments given in class. I was able to see this behavior firsthand during my interview of Renee, when she talked about certain aspects of the abuse, including how her parents responded when they found her sister in her room, humping her.

After explaining to Janelle and Leslie that Renee's behaviors were her way of expressing that she was not feeling safe while talking or responding to questions about things that made her feel powerless, they were able to change the ways in which they would typically talk to her. Instead of their responses sounding disciplinary in nature, they chose to change the way they spoke/talked to Renee so that they were being more understanding. They also modified the types of questions they asked. For example, they might ask "What help do you need to get your homework done?" instead of "Why didn't you do your homework?"

The bottom line here is that, in order to feel safer and more secure, Renee had to personify something else. She was presenting herself in a way that felt less threatening. She also acted younger than her chronological age, because she was reverting back to a time in which she felt safer, before the abuse started. Renee's clinginess had to do with not feeling safe as well. All of this was her way of expressing her fear of being alone – and of not feeling secure.

Of course, every child is different, and the child who discloses to you may exhibit other uncharacteristic behaviors following abuse, such as being rebellious, more withdrawn, more emotional… really, it could be anything that makes you stop and say, "That's not like my baby." These types of behaviors are likely all signs that your child has not forgotten about what happened. He or she is simply trying to deal with his or her memories about the abuse and what they represent. Scolding or trying to correct these behaviors will not get you the result you are seeking.

You may also notice your child directing anger toward you, which can be especially difficult. You may even feel like you deserve it, if you believe that you "allowed" – or minimally, that you did not prevent – the abuse that happened to your child.

What's important to remember here is that your child's feelings are starting to come out without her conscious awareness of them. You might have even asked your child why she is so angry, and in particular, angry at you. Please know that the likelihood of her having an answer to that question is slim to none. Most likely, she will say, "I don't know." And she is being truthful! She is probably aware that she is feeling that anger, but does not necessarily understand why. It is not uncommon for children to direct angry feelings at the person in their lives who is safest, because again, there is much less risk for them than there is for the child to be angry at someone else. Your child feels safer when she directs anger toward you, someone who will not stop loving or supporting her, or abandon her, no matter what. Again, this is not a conscious effort she is making, but more a result of the inner turmoil she feels, as well as the frustration resulting from her inability to change what happened to her, or make it go away.

While it may be a challenge to respond calmly and respectfully when your child is directing anger at you, it is going to be much more advantageous for you to do so, as opposed to letting your frustrations get the best of you. Not only will you reinforce for your child that angry feelings are okay, but you will also demonstrate to her that you do not have to respond in kind. Now, I'm certainly not advising you take verbal abuse from your child. I'm simply saying that this is one more teaching opportunity you can use to show her how to deal with inner turmoil. Allow her a cooling off period, and then, when you are both calm, begin to talk about her feelings. You don't necessarily need to ask why she is having the feelings, but focus instead on how to most appropriately deal with them.

CHAPTER 10:
MY CHILD IS ACTING... DIFFERENT.
(DON'T WORRY, IT'S STILL NORMAL!)

It is not uncommon for children and adults alike to be confused by behaviors uncharacteristic to the child.

In addition to what we've already covered, some different behaviors that may be exhibited by children who have experienced abuse may include, but are not limited to:

- Smearing feces on the wall.
- Hiding underwear with fecal stains or dried up feces.
- Urination in places other than the bathroom, such as in a bedroom.
- Hoarding of items like food, clothes, toys, etc.
- Hurting animals
- Starting fires

It is *crucial* to remember that your child is not misbehaving "on purpose."

These behaviors are ways in which your child's mind and body are trying to make sense of – or "fix" – what has happened and the resulting unsafe, insecure feelings.

As a parent, you *never* want to shame your child for these behaviors. Telling your child she is acting like a baby when she pees or poops her pants, and reminding her that she "knows better" won't work to end the behavior. It certainly won't work to tell her you are going to tell her friends what a baby she is, or other types of "shaming." Asking your child why she is doing this will do nothing more than cause you both more frustration.

She is not capable of explaining why. All she knows is the shame from doing such behaviors, which is a reflection of the shame she feels regarding the abuse, and it can be intensified by an improper response from a parent/adult. Believe me when I say, your child has felt more than enough shame. Children, like adults, try to return to a sense of certainty and normalcy after trauma or pain; however, they do not have the same knowledge and coping skills to deal with the abuse and its aftereffects.

So how do you deal with unsettling behavior resulting from abuse?

First, taking your child to therapy can help this process along.

Second, supporting your child unconditionally during this time is critical. Talking to your child about the changes you are seeing and asking if he/she feels safe may be a good start. Ask if there is something you or someone else can do to help your child feel safe. You may try a response like the following: "We are going to work through this together. I won't be mad at you, but I need you to tell me when you have an accident so we can help you get through this." The overarching message here is that you support her, and she is not alone.

Third, keeping the line of communication open after the investigation can assist in alleviating some of these behaviors. This does not mean forcing your child to talk. However, it is important to continue taking opportunities to discuss her feelings and thoughts about the abuse.

I don't want you to constantly bring it up, but you can, on occasion, have "discussion time" where you and your child can discuss/ask anything you/she would like. Do your best to frame this "discussion time" as a positive experience.

Don't present it as an open-ended discussion that might bring additional anxiety to your child. Think of it like this: If your boss has ever said something like, "We need to talk so come by my office this afternoon," you may have then spent the entire morning repeatedly analyzing in your head what you possibly did wrong to upset your boss. This is not the type of environment you are looking to create with a child who is already anxious.

Now if your boss said something like, "Hey, let's chat later this afternoon because I want to discuss some things I've been thinking about on your project and get your feedback," it's a totally different scenario, and you probably have a completely different mindset. In this scenario, you are "in the know" about what your boss wants to discuss, and you feel much more confident and safe having the discussion.

With this in mind, consider bringing up the "discussion time" by saying something like, "Hey, I just want some of your time later to check in with you, to see how you're feeling, and understand what more I might be able to do to help and support you." Again, you do not want this to continue in any particular routine per se. You want it to feel natural, yet regular enough that your child starts to learn that it's okay – that it's safe

– to tell you things. Ultimately, this will make your connection even stronger.

Trust your intuition when it comes to knowing when to initiate "discussion time." You may feel anxious or worried that by instigating the discussion, you are just going to cause your child more pain, but remember the pain is definitely already there. What you are actually doing is providing him the opportunity to process it and let it out, to keep it from festering inside and causing him even more damage in the long run.

Plus, you can use the discussions to reinforce and build upon your child's strengths, as he learns how to have an "external" voice about the abuse.

For example, if your child likes to write or journal, she may feel more comfortable writing out her thoughts and feelings first, and then discussing them after. Or, if your child likes to draw, you can encourage him to draw, which may help him better generate discussion points. Again, you are not forcing, but encouraging different opportunities to bring her thoughts out of her mind and into the open. These "distancing" (i.e. writing, drawing, etc.) behaviors can sometimes provide enough of a "buffer" that your child feels safer in discussing their thoughts and feelings about what happened.

Wondering how you will know how often or long to continue the discussion times? Again, trust your intuition. You will both know when it feels like "enough". This is not something to be dreaded, or that we want to turn into an "I'm tired of talking about it" type of thing. What we're going for here is "I'm feeling better about me." For example, maybe in your latest discussion time, your child tells you verbally that she really is feeling better and does not have anything more to say about the abuse. This is fine, but I encourage you to then watch her nonverbal communications (expressions and behaviors) to determine if they reinforce her words. Also, trust in her, yes. But also trust your parenting instinct. I can tell you that ignoring behaviors, feelings, and thoughts while maintaining silence will bring you and your child more grief and lead to greater misunderstandings about the abuse and what it means.

External Processing

Sometimes children exhibit what can be known as "external processing". This occurs when, seemingly out of nowhere, the child may say something – a specific word or phrase – that does not "fit" the moment.

Let's say, for example, that you're driving somewhere when suddenly, your child exclaims, "No, do it like this." Now when you hear this, the only two people in the car are you and your daughter. You ask her to whom she is talking and she appears startled. She may try to make up an excuse like, "I was just singing," or even deny that she said it at all because she truly may not even realize she did. Rest assured, your daughter more than likely is NOT experiencing psychosis. She is not crazy, nor is she hearing or seeing delusions. What is actually going on is that she is dealing with her memories of what happened, and trying to stop the thoughts and feelings that have intruded on her in that moment. So as the thoughts come into her head, in an effort to stop them, she may express things externally while her brain is replaying what happened, or certain conversations that had taken place.

Once, I interviewed a mother and father before interviewing their 7-year-old son, Christian, and they explained to me how Christian had recently developed what they described as a "tic." They stated Christian would be doing any number of activities (playing cards, games, bathing, doing homework, etc.) and would suddenly start blurting out what seemed like random phrases such as, "You idiot," "How can I," "No you say it that way," and "Well, not to me." They were trying to make sense of all these random comments, reading into each of them. What they didn't understand was that these outbursts were likely Christian's way of externalizing the conversations and messages that were going on routinely in his head. Again, this was not him experiencing auditory hallucinations (hearing someone who is not really tell him to do something). It was simply his brain's way of trying to come to terms with the abuse, and process the information. Once Christian's parents had this understanding, they were able to help "normalize" his feelings, by reassuring him he was not crazy and helping him understand it was his brain's way of helping him deal with the emotions and thoughts he had about the abuse. They also helped him by getting him to acknowledge (and they sometimes helped him correct) his thoughts and beliefs about the abuse. That's when they noticed his "externalizing" behaviors started to decrease.

CHAPTER 11:
GETTING HELP FOR MY CHILD

Counseling or therapy is certainly one of the venues that can be very successful in helping your child put his or her memories (and the thoughts and emotions that accompany them) into a better place in the brain in order to access and perceive them more appropriately and adeptly. Just as it is with "discussion times," there are no set guidelines for how long therapy should take to achieve healing, because it will depend upon the extent of the abuse, the response to the abuse, your child's perception of the abuse, and various other factors which can influence your child's healing process.

Children, similar to adults, need to process or make sense of the memories of the abuse, as well as the thoughts and emotions tied to them, in order to move past the trauma. For younger kids, play therapy is a great tool to help them do this. For older kids, much like adults, group therapy can prove to be very beneficial as well. Talking with a peer who has had similar experiences and who deals with similar thoughts and feelings can be very affirming for a child, and is generally much more effective than an adult telling the child how to feel. This does not discount the value of individual therapy with a trained, experienced counselor specializing in sexual abuse and trauma. This too can of course be extremely beneficial.

And don't worry if you fear that therapy will just cause the memories of the abuse to resurface again and again. Your child *will* experience the memories, and therapy allows him to put them into perspective while empowering your child to have more control over the intrusive thoughts and memories. Once you, your child, and the therapist start to see a change in behaviors, feelings, and thought patterns, you can decide together if it is time to terminate therapy.

Keep in mind that therapy sometimes is best received at different points in time during the healing process. For example, if a child is eight years old at the time therapy is initiated and he goes for a year, it does not necessarily mean he will never need to go again. It may be that when he reaches adolescence, things start changing for him: not just hormonally, but also in his greater knowledge and understanding of the abuse. This may prompt him to question his sexuality or his bodily functions. It is important for him to get the proper understanding of what abuse means and does not mean – that it is not representative of who he is, or his sexuality. He needs to know that this was an experience he had that does NOT have to negatively impact his behaviors or his feelings about himself. Even as an adult, when he becomes a father, he may start to question if he is safe or can be trusted around his child. He may start to believe the myth that if a child is abused, that child will then become an abuser. This is simply not the case, but these feelings and questions need to be addressed. It is much too stressful to carry this burden alone, and therapy may be the answer.

Children do not necessarily forget about abuse, but they can reorganize the thoughts and feelings tied to their memories of the abuse so that there is a greater sense of power and control. If children do not receive help and support after what can be a traumatic event like abuse, their thoughts and feelings about it can spiral out of control as they get caught up in negative self-talk, self-harming behaviors, and most detrimentally, low self-esteem. These maladaptive traits can lead to depression, anxiety, harmful relationships, and other harmful and unproductive life choices like substance abuse and dependence.

But it doesn't have to be that way. Children who have been abused can absolutely grow up to lead productive, successful lives.

In fact, numerous successful adults have been victims of childhood abuse, particularly childhood sexual abuse. Santana, Oprah, Tyler Perry, Maya Angelou, and Senator Scott Brown have not only gone through it, but they've also chosen to not be silent about it. They have each found their voice.

Your child is a survivor of abuse, as well, and he or she can definitely thrive.

In the next chapter, we cover exactly how to talk to your child, so you can help him or her do so.

CHAPTER 12:
HOW DO I TALK TO MY CHILD?

At this point, you may be thinking, "Okay, I understand the importance of my role in my child's healing. But what if I say the "wrong" thing?"

You're not alone. Once a child has disclosed abuse, it's not uncommon for the adult to struggle with knowing what to say or how to discuss the topic in the future. You want to say the "right" thing, the healing thing, the thing that is going to make it all better. That's what parents are supposed to do, right?

Actually, I'll say it again because it bears repeating: the best thing you can do is to simply *be there* for your child.

You can:

- Listen when she wants to talk, and respect when she doesn't.
- Randomly offer him a hug.
- Simply provide your company – sit with her in silence.
- Draw, read, or write with him.
- Play a board game with her.

See where I'm going with this? Whatever it may be, you don't have to say the "right" thing. Oftentimes, your child just needs to be heard, to know you're truly listening to her. We are such multitaskers these days that the simple, powerful act of *listening* gets underrated and overlooked. When your child starts talking to you about what happened, she's already shown a great deal of courage. The simple act of actively listening is one very effective way to let her know you want to listen to her and to respect what she has to say. Note: Active listening is not just sitting patiently without ever speaking. It's about routinely acknowledging what your child is saying, and checking your understanding of what she has said through repeating what you heard her say.

So let's say your child asks if she can talk to you about what happened. You only need to listen and affirm. Again, this does not mean you have to say "just the right thing." You do, however, need to listen with interest and concern. You're not there to judge her thoughts and feelings. The feelings are hers, and are neither right or wrong. Her thoughts, however, may need some work, but that's best to leave to a trained therapist. *You* don't need to be her therapist. Your job is to be a supportive, reliable, solid sounding board.

Once, while interviewing Nadine, a teenager, about her sexual abuse, she described how before she finally disclosed what had happened, her mother would constantly ask her what was wrong, and she would just remain silent. She talked about how she did not know how to put into words all the things that were wrong, in addition to the abuse. She explained how difficult it was to find the words even to discuss the abuse with her mother. Plus, she worried her mother wouldn't be able to handle it. Like most children, Nadine wanted to protect her mother, and did not know how to start a conversation about her experiences.

It is likely that the child who discloses to you will have similar misperceptions. Letting her know that she can talk to you about anything is a start, but expressing to her how, while you may have feelings about what she is telling you, it will never change your love for – and support of – her. This is what she really needs to feel safe enough to talk about her experiences. Saying something like, "When you tell me certain things, I may feel angry or sad, but it is not directed at you. Those are my feelings, neither right nor wrong. Just like you, I may need some time to process what you're telling me and I may have different feelings about it as I try to understand what you are telling me. This does not mean that what you told me is wrong or bad at all. I just need to figure out and understand for myself what has happened, so I know how to best support you."

Here's another example of an effective way of discussing abuse with a child:

Say a child tells you that, while she knows the abuse was not her fault, that there are times when she thinks, "If only I wouldn't have worn that outfit..." Feelings of confusion or guilt or the misattribution of her behaviors (wearing/choosing particular clothes are what caused her to be abused) are quite normal. Talking this out would be helpful to the child. Again, you do not have to be a therapist, just use your parental instinct to reassure her and help her understand she did not have responsibility for her abuse. She must understand that her actions did not cause the abuse. The way she dressed, the way she looked, the things she may have said (or not said), or any other behavior on her part did not cause the abuse.

Model for her how to put the responsibility where it belongs: the person who abused her was in full control of all manipulations that allowed the abuse to take place. This includes manipulations that may have even involved you, the parent. Thus, modeling can sound like this: "You know I thought that it was my fault because I brought Richard (the abuser) into our home, around you, and trusted him to be with you, one of the most important people to me in the whole world. I too had to learn though that I did not understand or see at first how he tricked me, tricked us, into trusting him so that he could hurt you."

This is where active listening can be SO helpful. Even if you don't understand something, affirm what your child is saying, which helps tremendously. Phrases like: "I can only imagine how that must have been for you/felt to you," and "I'm sorry you had to go through that alone at that time, but I'm here now and will help you in any way I can" go a long way with children.

So focus on letting your child know that you are there, that you're listening, and that you will be with her throughout the entire process. Help her understand that you will not tell her how she should feel, but will listen, and do the best you can to understand her thoughts and feelings.

Next up, we address the "elephant in the room": your perceived "failure" as a parent in the wake of a child's abuse.

SECTION 4:
THE SEXUAL ABUSE DISCLOSURE'S IMPACT ON YOU

CHAPTER 13:
AM I A FAILURE? AM I A BAD PARENT?

When a child is abused, it can impact every relationship the child has.

This impact can be felt in many ways, including how you talk to your child, how you interact with your child, the activities you do as a family, and how you feel about yourself.

Know that it is totally normal for you to question yourself, and what it all means about you and your parenting skills. There are several layers to these types of questions, and to understand them, remember that you are a secondary victim.

You have been adversely affected by the victimization of a child.

What happened is not your fault. You may feel like it is, because you somehow failed your child. But we all know there is no perfect parent. No matter how much we may strive to be one, perfection does not exist. Therefore, at a minimum, we want to do things differently or better than our own parents did.

Think back to your parents as you were growing up. You may not have ever questioned their parenting skills, but I bet there were times when you knew they were wrong in something they said or did. Did you confront your parents about it? Or did you just sort of "go with it," because you knew your parents were "supposed" to be right, no matter what?

Parents do not have all the answers. They are not perfect, and neither are you. The best we can do is model for our children the power of forgiveness and acceptance.

When I was a teenager, I remember asking my mom what a word meant. She told me to look it up in the dictionary, because I would remember it longer if I found the definition myself. Plus, that's what her mother told her to do, when she was growing up. I remember being so frustrated with her for withholding information from me. I just wanted her to tell me! Of course, I looked it up begrudgingly.

What I later learned from my mom was that she did not know what that word meant either, but she didn't want to admit that to me because she didn't want me to think of her as dumb. Now, my teenage behaviors and smart aleck responses may have given her the impression that I might think that, but what my mom didn't know was that I would never consider her dumb. Quite the contrary. My mom is one of the smartest women I've ever known. Her lack of knowledge in this one area didn't change the fact that she is my mother, and I respect her regardless of the fact that I now knew she did NOT have all the answers, all the time.

So letting your kids know you don't have all the answers – but that you will always do your best to be there for them, supporting them and helping them find answers – gives children the ability to have a more realistic view of their parents and adults, while still allowing them to maintain their sense of safety and security. (It also gets you 'off the hook' so to speak for always knowing the right thing to do or say!)

Plus, often times, when a child is developing a relationship with someone who abuses him, there is a simultaneous relationship the abuser builds with you. That means trust, and sometimes dependence, is not only developed, but also reinforced within the relationship. Allowing your child to do things with the abuser alone, letting the abuser keep your child overnight, or any opportunity the abuser presents to continue building the relationship was all manipulated by the abuser. The reinforcement of a perceived trust and dependence is what may prevent you from developing suspicions based on your intuition, or to push aside concerns you may have had for things that were said or done that you would have normally noticed.

This does not make you a bad parent.

This does make you human… and again, the secondary victim. So, before you go beating yourself up about "allowing" the abuse to happen, and/or for trusting someone you should not have, please remember abuse, particularly sexual abuse, is insidious, happening little by little over time, and typically occurs with someone loved and trusted.

Now, I realize it may be difficult for you to get past your feelings of guilt. You may find yourself replaying conversations or actions that NOW, knowing what you know, allow you to see the manipulations that provided the opportunity for abuse. Again, this does not mean you are inadequate or inept as a parent. It means that you are now using your experience, albeit difficult, to grow. You will build a stronger, greater sense of awareness when it comes to who you choose (and allow) to have a relationship with your child.

Think of it this way:

Have you ever been driving, and as you begin moving into the next lane, you quickly learn that another car was already in that lane, based on the blaring horn? You just didn't see it. I'd imagine that the next time you tried to change lanes, you were even more thorough in checking and verifying that it was safe to move over.

You probably didn't just stop driving from that point forward. Instead, you used that experience to guide you the next time around, and to keep you safe.

The same can be said of the abuse experience. You can now nurture a renewed sense of safety and trust that can go a long way in establishing lifelong secure attachments between you and your child. You can actually provide a greater sense of security to your child who may no longer trust anyone by helping him to find a new way to learn whom to trust, with what, and when.

While it may seem like sheltering your child is the only way to keep her safe, it's actually not productive or effective. First, trying to overcompensate by not allowing her to go places or be around people you have not "thoroughly" investigated can lull you into a false sense of security. Second, it tends to make the child feel as though she is being punished and isolated, which can lead to even more emotional and behavioral problems.

While working with a stay-at-home mom who had just begun a job and decided to let her five-year-old, Amanda, go to a daycare three times a week, the mom revealed to me an extreme amount of guilt over allowing Amanda out of her care. She expressed how she had been very wary of taking the job in the first place, because she had never let Amanda out of her or her immediate family's care.

After the first week of daycare, Amanda came home and told her mother how one of the "teachers" was touching her "pee pee." The guilt her mother carried was so great that it prevented her from trusting anyone alone with Amanda for quite some time. However, the next school year, Amanda was set to begin Kindergarten, and the mom was even more worried about it because Amanda had started exhibiting some behavioral issues like being extra clingy, crying over the smallest things (which had not previously been an issue), and bedwetting.

Through the course of therapy, these issues were resolved, but that resolution didn't come until Amanda's mom was able to deal with – and dispel – her overwhelming feelings of guilt that the abuse had been her fault. It was her challenge to allay her fears that her baby would be hurt again, and she would not be able to protect her. She had to accept that the abuse was not her responsibility, nor her fault, but that it was something she and Amanda would have to learn to overcome. As she came to understand this and trust her parenting skills and instincts more, she gained a more realistic sense of the power she did have as a parent, and Amanda's troubling behaviors began to slowly disappear.

Realize too that it is impossible to control everything in your child's life, no matter how much you want to protect her. Their interactions and connections with others are theirs, not yours, and those connections are inevitable.

What you *can* do is keep the lines of communication open. This does not mean becoming overbearing, forcing your child to tell you every detail of every moment. It does mean having and showing a genuine interest in what/how your child feels about others, situations, or relationships he may have with family members and friends. Truly respecting what your child has to say and valuing his opinions on these things go a long way in building a stronger relationship.

While helping your child heal from the fallout of abuse, you will be continually modeling for her through your actions. She will constantly seek direction from you, even when you don't think she is paying any attention to you at all.

Trying to hold back your emotions is not necessarily helpful, as it ends up demonstrating to your child that emotions are too painful to be dealt with, so she should push them away and pretend to be in control. This of course is an extremely unhealthy way of dealing with emotions, and perpetuates more difficulties. For example, when a child first tells you of her abuse, you may fiercely hold back your tears. Well, just as you know your child, she knows you. So trying to hide the tears isn't really serving the purpose you may think it is. Your child may receive the message that when something bothers you or hurts you, you are to just keep it inside, not letting anything out. Now your child learns that people are not supposed to show their feelings, or even have them.

Again, you are human, and it's okay to show emotion. This does not make you weak or incapable. (Note: I'm of course not suggesting you sob or rage uncontrollably, putting your child in the position of having to take care of you and your feelings. It does, however, mean that showing emotion can model for your child that you have feelings too, and that the sharing of them is a healthy step toward releasing them.)

Remember, you are your child's best parent/role model when you are able to incorporate those traits and allow your child an open venue to talk about things that may be very difficult, scary, or confusing.

And this makes you an *excellent* parent or guardian, and keeps your child safe.

CHAPTER 14:
IT'S TIME TO TAKE CARE OF YOU

It's hard enough raising a child. When a child is abused, it makes it that much more difficult.

More and more research on the effects of abuse, from mental health to our physical well-being, seems to surface daily. There is even more research on depression, blood pressure, and even some types of cancer being linked to childhood abuse. While some of these things may not be reversible, they are manageable.

The earlier you begin working on healing from this trauma, the better. Today is a great time to start! Breaking old patterns and habits of dealing with traumatic events in an unhealthy way takes much effort, but the payoff is absolutely more than worth it.

What to Do Now

It is only through connecting with a strong, trustworthy support system, and having the ability to communicate your thoughts and feelings about what has happened, that you will move forward in your healing.

Seeking your own support is crucial. Like most things in life, families are a top down organization. If things are stable and going well at the top of the family system, then there is a trickle-down effect, and things are therefore stable and well at the bottom, too.

You've probably heard the saying, "You can't take care of anyone else if you don't take care of yourself first." This statement rings true on a number of levels. First, just as you want to take care of your child, your child wants to take care of you; however, as we know, this is not the way it's supposed to go. Parents are supposed to take care of children. Period, end of story. To do this effectively, you too are going to need a strong support system. I'm not talking about posting your (or your child's) feelings or thoughts about what happened on social media to garner support or suggestions on what to do, which is another violation of your child's trust. I am talking about having or getting someone in your life with whom you can have true "intimacy." My dear friend Marina calls this concept the "into me you see," and it's a perfect description of intimacy. You are going to need someone who can listen to your innermost fears, worries, concerns, confusion and anything else you throw at her or him without judgment.

Having a sounding board, a source of supportive listening, and a trustworthy person who cares can mean the difference between being the supportive parent/guardian/adult you want to be, and the one incapable of attending to your child's needs. Choose people you know have been previously supportive to you during a rough time, and who you know will not air your intimate thoughts with others.

You may want to check with your child's therapist as to the availability of parent support groups. These groups, comprised of parents who are going through similar situations as you, are often one of the most effective and efficient ways of helping you get through the secondary trauma that can arise from abuse to your child.

When you have this for yourself, you will notice that your interactions, including with your child regarding the abuse, will actually feel more meaningful and beneficial.

What you absolutely want to avoid is the following:

First, don't discuss any of your child's issues with others in front of him, including in phone conversations. You may think you're being quiet, and he won't hear you, but there is actual research showing how we can hear our names being said from a great distance, even when we can't make out other words from that same distance. Add that to a child's natural curiosity and inclination to be sneaky when adults are talking, and you have the perfect opportunity for him to overhear you talking about him, and possibly misunderstanding or misinterpreting what you are saying. This can be disastrous, so be sure to be cautious.

Second, at all costs, avoid adding to the abused child's hardship by making him feel like he has to take care of you, or "protect" you from things like his feelings, thoughts or experiences in relation to the abuse. Remember, you're allowed – and I encourage you – to share your feelings. Of course you're feeling them: anger, fear, confusion. (Sound familiar?) So, model healthy behaviors, for your child. Doing so is one of the best ways to help her move forward, and become the productive adult you know she can be.

Show her how to express her feelings in a healthy way, in a safe, comfortable environment. It is okay to let your child know that you have feelings about what happened to her, but that it is not her job to try and control or "fix" those emotions. Saying something like, "You can tell me anything, even if you're afraid it will make me mad, sad or scared. That is okay. My feelings are mine and help me to get things out instead of keeping stuff on the inside (like my stomach in knots or a lump in my throat)." This way, you're demonstrating that feelings are neither good nor bad, and that you are capable of handling them... and your child will learn to express ALL the feelings she feels on the inside in a more productive, helpful manner.

You can also let your child know that your feelings of love for him will never change, no matter what he tells you or how you feel about what he has said. There is a big difference in feeling angry or hurt that abuse has happened to your child and your child believing you will be mad at him for what happened to him. Kids though, don't always get that distinction. You, the parent/adult, can spell it out for them.

You, your child, your family, and your community can heal and become stronger after abuse. As mentioned previously, taking care of yourself is the first essential step in doing so, so that you are able to effectively take care of your child in the face of abuse.

Remember, families and communities that can heal together are not only stronger, but wiser and better adept at facing a world of uncertainty, which can sometimes be filled with tragedy.

Finally, abuse does not have to define you or the abused. It can be a traumatic event that, when handled appropriately, can provide us with life lessons to help us through future difficult times. Utilizing your resources, like appropriate support systems, counseling, victim advocates, and the like will make the journey one of hope and healing, instead of hopelessness and despair.

CHAPTER 15:
DEALING WITH YOUR CHILD'S ANGER

When a child is unable to process his or her anger in a healthy way, you can provide him or her with safe exercises like the following to help him do so. Be sure to explain beforehand the purpose of the exercises, and what is going to happen before doing the exercise, so your child understands the benefit and expectations in advance.

Exercise One: The Ice Bucket

Fill a bucket with ice. In a safe area, where nothing and no one could get hurt, have the child throw out each piece of ice, one-by-one, against a stone or brick wall, or really, any hard surface. Then, once the bucket is empty, watch the pieces of broken ice melt away.

Use this exercise as a metaphor to show your child how feelings are just like the ice – once they are felt, you can let them melt away.

Exercise Two: Picking up the Pieces

Get a large catalog or group of papers, and encourage the child to destroy them, essentially ripping them to shreds. Do NOT have him/her clean it up immediately once this is done. The goal here is to allow the child to sit with the pieces around him for as long as he wants, and when the child is ready, THEN it gets cleaned up. I encourage you to lend a hand in the clean-up process, to show her how you are always there to help her pick up the pieces and contain them once again.

These are just some of the exercises you can do with your child to help her better understand how to deal with her feelings of anger. Anger is neither good nor bad; it is simply a feeling, and a powerful one at that. Remember, no one likes to feel powerless, so allowing your child to feel the anger and express it in a more purposeful way can help you and your child become empowered.

SECTION 5:
HELPFUL TIDBITS

CHAPTER 16:
EXPLANATIONS OF WHICH
PROFESSIONALS MAY BE INVOLVED

As you're going through this process, you may encounter the following professionals. Remember they're here to help you and your child!

Child Protective Services:
Responsible for determining child safety needs and providing resources to ensure those needs are met.

Counselor or Therapist:
Responsible for helping you and your child heal emotionally after abuse occurs.

Dedicated Forensic Interviewer:
Responsible for listening and asking your child developmentally appropriate and sensitive questions about the allegation without leading or suggesting to your child what may have happened.

Law Enforcement:

Patrol Officer: Person who gets basic, initial information on the allegations.

Detective: Person who handles your case from beginning to end.

Prosecutor:

Responsible for determining if a case will go forward through the court system and preparing you and your child accordingly.

Judge and Jury:

Responsible for weighing the evidence presented in a case to determine guilt or innocence and penalty.

Victim Advocate/Crisis Intervention Specialist:

Responsible for keeping you informed about the legal process and providing you with information and resources to help you and your family throughout the case.

CHAPTER 17:
QUESTIONS FOR FINDING THE
APPROPRIATE THERAPIST

Searching for the right therapist does not have to be a daunting task. Victim Advocates and Crisis Intervention Specialists (especially those located in Advocacy Centers), and Dedicated Forensic Interviewers, are very adept at helping you with this task. You will still have to do the interviewing, so to speak, but never feel as though you have to go into this blind. Below are some helpful interview questions, which should provide you with the necessary information to make an educated choice of counselors.

In what specific area is your training and work experience? Do you have experience working with adolescents/pre-teens/preschoolers? Children with special needs? What kind of experience do you have (from college, work experience, workshops or training courses)?

The type of answer you are looking for here is that the therapist spends most of her educational training (usually about 20 hours a year) in the field of abuse and in trauma. There are national conferences, local trainings, and online courses that provide this. You are looking to see if the therapist has a well-rounded source for learning.

What is your area of specialty? How much training have you received in this area?

What you want to hear is that sexual abuse, physical abuse and neglect are her/his primary areas of expertise and workload. S/he should be receiving a minimum of 12 hours of training per year in this area of expertise.

How long have you been licensed?

Typically, you want someone who has been in the child abuse field (sexual, physical abuse and neglect) for a minimum of five years. Now, if the therapist's training/internship was with a facility which solely specialized in child abuse, you may consider this training in her/his years of experience.

Have you ever had a complaint filed against you?

If her answer is yes, this is not necessarily a deal-breaker. You want to find out how she handles her disclosure of this (along with doing your own research online with the Board of Behavioral Health) and what the complaint actually was, what she had to do to resolve the issue, and if it were a sustainable complaint (proven).

Did you practice in another state? Which one(s)?

Again, what you're looking for is if there were any complaints filed against this therapist elsewhere, and how they were resolved, if there were.

How do you keep yourself updated on the latest counseling techniques?

Here you are trying to find out if the therapist keeps up-to-date with the latest research, participates in supervision, or belongs to organizations (APSAC, ATSA, ISPCAN) which provide her with the latest techniques and research in this field.

- American Professional Society on the Abuse of Children (APSAC)
- Association on the Treatment of Sexual Abusers (ATSA)
- International Society on the Prevention of Child Abuse and Neglect (ISPCAN)

What percentage of your clientele are adolescents or preteens or preschoolers? Sexual abuse victims? Have special needs?

The answer you're looking for should be over 50% for whichever age range or special need your child is presently in.

How involved are we (parents) in the counseling? Will my child's privacy be respected? When are things not private and confidential?

Typically, the therapist should be including you in the beginning of the session, talking to you without your child to determine how the past week has been going, if there were any significant changes or issues. You do not want to meet with the therapist after your child's session so that your child feels secure in what s/he has just done in session and her privacy is maintained. What cannot be considered confidential is any information provided by your child regarding danger to self or danger to others.

How often will my child need to meet with you? Where?

Sessions are typically 50 minutes in duration and should occur weekly. Sessions should not be spread out to every two weeks until enough work has been successfully completed and the plan is to start terminating counseling services per the therapist's and your child's evaluation. You also don't want to meet more frequently than once a week as this type of work gets to be too intense for your child. The specialized counseling on abuse should never take place in your home as this should be your child's safe place and retreat.

Above all, as a parent **remember to trust your instincts. If it doesn't feel right, then it is not a good fit.**

CHAPTER 18:
ADDITIONAL RESOURCES

This book serves as only one resource in guiding you through what can be a very trying time, but it is my hope that by reading the information and utilizing the resources provided in it, you will gain a realistic understanding of abuse (and the trauma which may accompany it), the reality of what it actually means for you and your family, and the systemic response to it.

You are the greatest mirror for success your child can have, and educating yourself with this book and other resources will certainly help you further that process.

Remember that knowledge is power, and we all want to feel powerful, especially in situations where we have felt a loss of it. Seeking and asking for help is not a sign of weakness, but one of true bravery and realistic expectations on the healing process.

Some of my favorite resources include:

For parents who were abused as children:
- Outgrowing the Pain by Eliana Gil, Ph.D.
- Outgrowing the Pain Together by Eliana Gil, Ph.D.

For understanding children's sexual behaviors and knowledge:
- Understanding Children's Sexual Behaviors by Toni Cavanagh Johnson, Ph.D. *(Also available in Spanish)*
- www.tcavjohn.com

National Center on the Sexual Behavior of Youth
- www.ncsby.org *(Also available in Spanish)*

For information about Advocacy Centers who can help you decide on what to do after your child discloses abuse:
- www.acfan.net *(In Arizona)*
- www.nationalchildrensalliance.org *(In the United States)*

For information about what to do when your child has been abused or how to prevent abuse:
- 1-800-4 A CHILD (1-800-422-4453) *Staffed by Master's Level Counseling Professionals*
- www.preventchildabuse.org
- www.stopitnow.org
- www.atsa.org

For information on at-risk children, youth and adults:
- www.nearipress.org

ABOUT THE AUTHOR

Growing up in the South with a very loving, close-knit family provided Chris the safety and security she needed to become a strong, independent woman.

However, the eye-opening experiences she had early on in her teaching, and then counseling careers, allowed her to hone her skills and knowledge necessary for listening to others' challenges. These experiences, paired with her solid foundation, gave her the ability to help others find the appropriate and much-needed support they sought so that their voices may be heard.

While she has helped victims and their families across the world, Chris makes her home and career in Arizona, where she lives with her husband, Kenneth.

Made in the USA
Columbia, SC
20 January 2018